FRANCHI
FEELS RIGHT

COOKBOOK
GAME ON

MARETTI
EDITORE

FRANCHI FOOD ACADEMY
COOKBOOK

Publishing director
Manfredi Nicolò Maretti

Editor in chief
Maria Paola Poponi

Graphic design
Maretti Editore
(Edoardo Maria Manuguerra)

Made and produced in Italy
Printing closed in December 2021

www.marettieditore.com
instagram: maretti_editore
facebook: maretti editore

ISBN 978-88-9397-034-1

SUMMARY

INDEX OF RECIPES

STARTER

FIRST COURSE

SECOND COURSE

PREFACE

Let's face it, traveling is one of the pleasures of life. Savor the thrill of discovery, the wonder of meeting new realities, the joy of looking up for a moment from your corner of the world and satisfying the curiosity that is part of the most easy-going side of us all.

But are you really sure that travelling necessarily means packing your suitcase, analyze an itinerary, take tickets and a map – or a smartphone perhaps – and jump on a plane?

And what if, on the other hand, to awaken the "little self" in us, all that was needed was a pinch of imagination, a good dose of creativity and a great passion?

This is what it takes to make simple moments of everyday life an unforgettable experience. And these are the main ingredients of Franchi Food Academy.

After six years of activity and many mouth-watering dishes, it has been called in many ways: academy, cooking school, restaurant, cooking show, cooking class, cooking contest...

But the question is: why limit yourself to one mere definition?

Franchi Food Academy is so much more. It's a life style, *from the nature to the table*, combining two great passions such as hunting and good food, while creating something new.

It is a vision of cooking aimed at enhancing game meat as a healthy raw material with major nutritional properties, through tantalizing recipes and with the pleasure of tasting them together.

It is the desire to spread a new culinary culture free of taboos, promoting the quality of raw materials, the importance of the game meat chain, the correct treatment of meat to enhance its unmistakable flavor.

And above all it is a network of chefs and enthusiasts from all over the world, who surprise us with their creations and, through original and innovative recipes, share their corner of the world and their idea of cooking with us.

This book offers fifty-two recipes, one for each weekend to be enjoyed in company, transporting us on an incredible culinary journey in which to savor, step by step, particular flavors and combinations.

What are we waiting for? Apron on and burning stove... off we go!

DISCOVERING THE CHEFS

ROBERTO DORMICCHI
ITALY

He loves to define himself as a chef and more. Passionate about sports and outdoor activities, teacher of a Marche cooking school, he lives a few kilometers from Acqualagna, the homeland of truffles, and has been in the culinary sector for about twenty years. He collaborates with numerous restaurants and colleagues, including Mauro Uliassi, whose influence has marked a real leap in quality in his professional growth. He was among the first to join the Franchi Food Academy network.

MICHAEL HUNTER
CANADA

Professional chef and lover of the outdoors, in 2015 he opens the acclaimed Antler restaurant in Toronto and in 2020 he publishes his first cookbook *The Hunter Chef Cookbook*, which wins the second prize of the Taste Canada Cookbook Awards, in the fall of 2021. Michael has been a proud Franchi hunter for 10 years.

GABRIEL JONSSON
SWEDEN

Love for food, hunting, fishing and days in contact with nature – that's how Gabriel describes himself. A dreamer, who in 2019 chose to change his life, leaving a secure job in the construction industry and dedicating himself to his greatest passion: cooking. The same year he participates and wins the edition of Swedish Master Chef, opening the doors to a life that until then was just a dream.

STEFANO MARINUCCI
ITALY

Author of numerous articles in specialized magazines and books in the sector, lecturer at Carpigiani Gelato University, over the years he has been the protagonist of several television programs on national networks. In 2014 he won the gold medal in the World Culinary Cup, thanks to a salt sculpture. Dog lover by passion, he keeps up the family culinary tradition, with choreographic dishes based on game.

IRIS ROSSI
ITALY

Daughter of restaurateurs and hunters, she literally grew up in the kitchen among the traditional family recipes, which she loves to creatively revisit in a modern way. Also, thanks to this passion, she is one of the founders of Franchi Food Academy, which she has been carrying forward with enthusiasm from day one.

VILLI TOSI
NEW ZEALAND

Growing up on a farm in New Zealand, the outdoors runs through his veins. Fishing and hunting are for him a real lifestyle, in which ethics and respect for nature are key values. Hence, Villi came up with the idea of filming some of his adventures and sharing them, with hunters and not only, on his Wild Meat Hunter NZ channel. Tidbits of experiences, from the moment of going out to the end of the day, which inevitably ends around a table, with a new game recipe.

WADE TRUONG
USA

Lifelong Virginian, he is a self-taught chef and hunter, who combines a passion for the table with a deep sense of gratitude towards the environment and the natural riches offered to us, to be protected and safeguarded. For Wade, every meal should be cherished and celebrated, meaningful and conscious, as a reminder of who we are, where we come from and where we are going.

NUTRITIONAL VALUES
#TASTERIGHT

VENISON

CARBOHYDRATE	0 g
PROTEIN	36,08 g
FAT	3,93 g
ENERGY	190 kcal

WILD BOAR

CARBOHYDRATE	0 g
PROTEIN	27,8 g
FAT	4,3 g
ENERGY	157 kcal

HARE

CARBOHYDRATE	0 g
PROTEIN	32,88 g
FAT	3,5 g
ENERGY	172 kcal

TURKEY

CARBOHYDRATE	0 g
PROTEIN	28,81 g
FAT	2,06 g
ENERGY	139 kcal

DUCK

CARBOHYDRATE	0 g
PROTEIN	23,38 g
FAT	11,15 g
ENERGY	200 kcal

MOOSE

CARBOHYDRATE	0 g
PROTEIN	29,15 g
FAT	0,97 g
ENERGY	133 kcal

QUAIL

CARBOHYDRATE	0 g
PROTEIN	25 g
FAT	14,04 g
ENERGY	226 kcal

GOOSE

CARBOHYDRATE	0 g
PROTEIN	25,06 g
FAT	21,83 g
ENERGY	304 kcal

BISON

CARBOHYDRATE	0 g
PROTEIN	28,32 g
FAT	2,41 g
ENERGY	142 kcal

PHEASANT

CARBOHYDRATE	0 g
PROTEIN	32,26 g
FAT	12,05 g
ENERGY	238 kcal

STORE BOUGHT MEAT

CHICKEN

CARBOHYDRATE	0,1 g
PROTEIN	25,07 g
FAT	10,65 g
ENERGY	196 kcal

BEEF

CARBOHYDRATE	0 g
PROTEIN	29,85 g
FAT	11,3 g
ENERGY	229 kcal

PORK

CARBOHYDRATE	0 g
PROTEIN	27,69 g
FAT	10,5 g
ENERGY	211 kcal

SALMON

CARBOHYDRATE	0,1 g
PROTEIN	25,08 g
FAT	9,06 g
ENERGY	188 kcal

(Average vaules based on 100 g of portion)
Source: US Department of Agricolture, Agricoltural Research Service

WILD GAME MEAT

The game is born free and lives in the wild in its own habitat. Here the animals are hunters and their lifestyle makes them build a lean and well-structured muscular system, with a variable associated with the species, sex, age and physiological conditions. Wild meat is absolutely natural presenting important nutritional values. Its marketing is controlled by the Wild Game Processors, in accordance with current legislation on hygiene and health quality. This ensures compliance with the supply chain and a product meeting food and safety standards.

Low in calories and cholesterol, the game is rich in iron, protein, zinc, vitamin B12 and Omega 3, with a favorable ratio Ω6/Ω3 fatty acids and has important organoleptic qualities.

As part of the *Selvatici e Buoni* project, carried out in the province of Bergamo in the three-year period 2017-2019 and supported by the UNA Foundation (Uomo Natura Ambiente), a specific chemical investigation was implemented on game samples taken during hunting activities, which allowed to define the nutritional values, according to ISO-coded analyzes. Game contains less fat than regular red meats. For the success of a recipe, you have to be careful with the hygienic treatment of the carcass and perform a correct aging process, a biochemical process thanks to which the muscle is transformed into meat, so to increase tenderness and digestibility, in a way that flavors are enhanced.

If properly processed after all phases, wild meats will strike with awe even the most refined palates; through new ways of cooking at low temperatures or raw preparations, you can enjoy their delicate flavor and enhance the local cuisine with a raw material of the highest quality.

Silvio Barbero
Vice-president of the Pollenzo University of Gastronomic Sciences Food Lab
Scientific coordinator of the *Selvatici e Buoni* project

Luca Pellicioli
Veterinarian
Scientific contact for the *Selvatici e Buoni* project

Serves
4

Difficulty
Low

Time
15'

Game
Roe deer

Calories
350 Kcal

Chef
Roberto Dormicchi

Wine
Montecucco Sangiovese DOCG

CANAPÉ WITH VENISON CARPACCIO

Preparation

Blend the mascarpone cheese with thyme, lemon zest, parmesan cheese, then season with salt and pepper. Cut the sliced bread into triangles and toast them.

Cut the fillet into slices and season with lemon juice, oil and pepper.

Spread the mascarpone cheese on the bread with a pastry bag using a star tip. Add the venison carpaccio on top and garnish with black truffle.

Ingredients

G 150 venison fillet
8 sliced bread
G 150 mascarpone cheese
G 30 grated parmesan cheese
G 30 black truffle
mL 20 extra virgin olive oil
Thyme to taste
Lemon zest to taste
Lemon juice to taste
Salt and pepper to taste

Serves
4

Difficulty
Medium

Time
30'

Game
Deer

Calories
660 Kcal

Chef
Roberto Dormicchi

Wine
Bramaterra DOC

PUFFED PASTA WITH POUNDED VENISON

Preparation

Cook the conchiglioni in plenty of salted water for about 30', let them boil slowly. Drain, lay on a drying tray, and bake at 40° C (104° F) for about 12 h.

Bring the temperature of the peanut oil up to 200° C (392° F); stir-fry the conchiglioni. Drain and arrange over the straw paper.

Pound the venison meat with knife, season with the chopped shallot, garlic, mustard, Worcestershire sauce, few drops of lemon, extra virgin olive oil, salt, and pepper.

Fill each conchiglione with the mixture. Serve with extra virgin olive oil and ground pepper.

Ingredients

G 300 venison meat
12 conchiglioni (large pasta shells)
mL 500 peanut oil
G 20 shallot
1 clove of garlic
G 10 mustard
Straw paper to taste
Lemon juice to taste
Worcestershire sauce to taste
Salt and pepper to taste
Extra virgin olive oil to taste

Serves
4

Difficulty
Medium

Time
8h

Game
Goose

Calories
233 Kcal

Chef
Wade Troung

Wine
Barbera d'Alba DOC

BOURBON GOOSE RILLETTE

Preparation

Rinse and pat dry the goose legs. Mix salt, sugar, instacure, and herbs together and cover the meat. Refrigerate for 8-12 h, or vacuum seal and refrigerate for 2 h.

Remove excess salt, place the meat in the Dutch oven and cover with the stock. Bring to a boil, cover, and cook over medium-low heat for about 4-6 h, until the meat is tender enough to pull away from the bone with a fork. Remove the meat, then allow it to drain and cool enough to handle.

Meanwhile, strain the braising liquid and melted fat through a fine-mesh strainer. Let cool and use a spoon to separate the cooled fat from the liquid. Save both the fat and the braising liquid.

Mince the meat by separating it from the bones, remove all cartilage and skin. Place the meat in a bowl and shred further with your hands. Season with a few pinches of pepper and a splash of bourbon. Add a splash of the reserved braising liquid and continue mixing. Add some of the reserved fat and mix.

Keep shredding the meat, until the rillette will take on a smooth, spreadable consistency. Add a little extra salt or pepper to taste. Spoon the rillette into jars, pat it down and top with a little goose fat to form a nice layer on top. Refrigerate without a lid, and once cooled, put a lid on it.

Serve with toast, something pickled, mustard, and any of your favorite charcuterie fixins.

Ingredients

G 1500 goose legs and thighs skin on
G 38 salt
G 38 sugar
G 4 instacure #1 (94% Kosher salt, 6% sodium nitrate)
2 sprigs rosemary
mL 75 stock unsalted
Thyme to taste
Bourbon to taste
Black pepper, freshly ground, coarse to taste

Serves
4

Difficulty
Medium

Time
30'

Game
Roe deer

Calories
230 Kcal

Chef
Roberto Dormicchi

Wine
Verdicchio di Matelica DOC

VENISON TARTARE WITH RICOTTA CHEESE AND EXOTIC SALAD

Ingredients

G 300 venison loin
G 20 tropea onion
G 5 anchovy fillets
G 5 salted capers
G 250 sheep ricotta
G 100 cucumber
G 100 celery
G 100 pineapple
G 50 rocket
1 green apple
Soy sauce to taste
Worcester sauce to taste
Mint to taste
Lime to taste
Salt and pepper to taste
Extra virgin olive oil to taste

Preparation

Remove all the ribbing and skin from the venison loin. Cut the meat with a knife to obtain small cubes.

Add the onion, capers previously washed and squeezed, and anchovy fillets all chopped finely. Season with soy sauce, Worcester sauce, fine salt, black pepper, and oil and refrigerate.

In a bowl, cream the ricotta cheese with salt, pepper, and oil. Clean and cut into small cubes pineapple and green apple, previously cleaned of skin and central parts, cucumber, and celery. Season with mint, lime zest and juice, pepper, fine salt, and oil.

Arrange the ricotta cream, tartare and exotic salad on the plate.

Serves
4

Difficulty
Low

Time
25'

Game
Fallow deer

Calories
374 Kcal

Chef
Iris Rossi

Wine
Campidano di Terralba DOC

Ingredients

G 120 venison fillet
G 150 fregola
G 100 basil pesto
G 200 yellow cherry tomatoes
G 100 feta cheese
Salt and pepper to taste
Extra virgin olive oil to taste

FREGOLA WITH VENISON PESTO, CHERRY TOMATOES AND FETA CHEESE

Preparation

Cook the fregola in boiling salted water according to the indicated cooking time. Drain and run under cold water to cool. Place the fregola in a bowl, add one or two tablespoons of extra virgin olive oil and stir. This procedure will prevent it from sticking.

Cut the feta into cubes and the previously washed cherry tomatoes into small cubes.

Add the pesto to the fregola and top with the tomatoes and cheese, mix well and set aside to flavor.

After having carefully cleaned and trimmed the fillet, preheat a frying pan with oil and coarse salt. Grill the meat on all sides over high heat, it should brown on the outside and remain pink in the center, making sure the inside is hot. Cut the fillet into bite-sized pieces.

Serve by placing the fregola on the plate and the venison on top.

Serves
4

Difficulty
Medium

Time
50'

Game
Wild boar

Calories
221 Kcal

Chef
Roberto Dormicchi

Wine
Vernaccia di Serrapetrona DOCG

JERUSALEM ARTICHOKE CREAM, WILD BOAR ROLL

Ingredients

G 100 slices of wild boar
G 300 Jerusalem artichoke
mL 50 extra virgin olive oil
mL 150 vegetable stock
G 30 sliced speck
G 100 fresh spinach
1 lemon
G 200 savoy cabbage
Sunflower oil for frying
Rosemary to taste
Salt and pepper to taste

Preparation

Clean the Jerusalem artichoke and keep the skins aside.

Dice the Jerusalem artichoke flesh and brown it with extra virgin olive oil, pour with vegetable stock and cook for 5'. Adjust the salt and pepper and blend using the immersion blender.

Sear the spinach in a pan with extra virgin olive oil.

Pound the slices of wild boar to tenderize, stuff them with salt, pepper, chopped rosemary, lemon zest, slices of speck and spinach. Roll them up and wrap them with food grade film.

Cook in water at 90° C (194° F) for 30'. Drain and leave to cool.

Sear the cabbage leaves in boiling water, drain and leave to cool. Cut the savoy cabbage into julienne, season with oil, salt and pepper.

Fry Jerusalem artichoke skins in boiling sunflower oil, drain and salt them.

Arrange the Jerusalem artichoke cream in the serving dish, the wild boar rolls cut into small pieces, and decorate with fried Jerusalem artichoke.

Serves
4

Difficulty
Medium

Time
2h

Game
Pheasant

Calories
199 Kcal

Chef
Stefano Marinucci

Wine
Dolcetto d'Alba DOC

PHEASANT IN JELLY WITH BLACK TRUFFLE

Ingredients

1 pheasant breast
1 white onion
2 medium carrots
G 50 celery
G 50 black truffle
G 25 gelatin powder
L 1 water
L 1 vegetable stock
mL 200 apple cider vinegar
Purple carrot powder (for decoration) to taste
Edible vegetables and flowers to taste
Salt and pepper to taste
Extra virgin olive oil to taste

Preparation

Put the breast in a bowl with a little oil, salt and pepper and a glass of apple cider vinegar, leaving it to flavor for about 1 h.

Next, drain and simmer with diced carrots, onion and celery. Always sprinkle with a little vegetable stock, salt and pepper everything.

When cooked, remove from heat and place in 6-7 cm molds, preferably glass. Heat the water with the gelatine and pour it into the mold.

Add the grated truffle in flakes, which will give that touch of originality and fragrance to the dish.

Once cooled, serve in a serving dish, decorating with edible flowers.

Serves
4

Difficulty
Low

Time
1h

Game
Pheasant

Calories
391 Kcal

Chef
Stefano Marinucci

Wine
Frascati Superiore Riserva DOCG

COUNTRY SALAD WITH PAPRIKA PHEASANT

Ingredients

G 250 pheasant breast
G 400 green salad
G 200 carrots
G 100 peas
G 100 avocado
G 100 red and yellow cherry tomatoes
G 100 baguette
G 100 goat yogurt
Paprika and coriander to taste
Salt and pepper to taste
Extra virgin olive oil to taste

Preparation

Place the pheasant breast inside a vacuum bag with oil, salt and paprika and condition. Leave to flavor for 30', then cook in a bain-marie for 30' at a temperature of 70° C (158° F).

Meanwhile, cut the bread into slices, season with oil and salt and toast it in a ventilated oven at a temperature of 120° C (248° F) for 10'.

Open the vacuum bag and cut the breast evenly, taking care not to dirty the inside with the red paprika.

Wash the vegetables, cut the carrots, tomatoes and salad, clean the avocado, boil the peas and let them cool.

Compose the dish with all the elements to your taste, using your imagination.

Season with goat yogurt, rich in calcium and phosphorus and add a little coriander to give freshness.

Serves
4

Difficulty
Low

Time
3h 15'

Game
Elk

Calories
416 Kcal

Chef
Michael Hunter

Wine
Amarone della Valpolicella
Classico DOCG

ELK LIVER
WITH CARAMELIZED ONIONS

Ingredients

G 450 liver cut in to 4 pieces
1 red onion
mL 250 red wine
G 130 sugar
mL 30 brandy or cognac
G 5 salt for brine
Butter to taste
Herbs to taste
Salt and pepper to taste
Extra virgin olive oil to taste

Preparation

Add the portions of liver to a container and cover with cold water. Add 1 teaspoon of salt to the water and liver. This will draw out excess blood from the liver and soften the gamey flavor. Soak overnight or for at least 3 h.

Add the wine and sugar to a small pot and boil to reduce by ¾ rds until it resembles a sticky sauce. Remove the liver from the water and pat dry.

Add the sliced onion to a small pot and sauté on high heat with a little oil and butter, cover with a lid and reduce to medium heat.

Stir onions occasionally, when translucent in color add 5 g of sugar and the brandy and reduce until almost dry. The onions should be soft and appear caramel in color after 10-15′ cooking.

Heat a large cast iron pan or heavy bottom frying pan on high heat. Add a little oil and season the liver with salt and pepper. Fry the liver in the oil and then add a little butter. Cook for 1-2′ per side.

Remove and rest for 2-3′ before slicing. Garnish with the caramelized onion, wine glaze and fresh herbs.

Serves
4

Difficulty
Medium

Time
50'

Game
Hare

Calories
335 Kcal

Chef
Stefano Marinucci

Wine
Franciacorta Rosé DOCG

HARE LIVER PATÉ ON CROUTONS AND FRESH FIGS

Ingredients

G 500 hare liver
2 fresh spring onions
G 50 butter
G 30 sugar
G 100 fresh figs
G 100 baguette
mL 100 vegetable stock
Walnuts to taste
Bay leaf and rosemary to taste
Cognac to taste
Salt and pepper to taste
Extra virgin olive oil to taste

Preparation

Thoroughly wash the hare liver under running water, dry, and cut into small pieces, then place them in a pan over medium heat.

Let it dry and then add the oil, bay leaf and rosemary, keep cooking for 10'.

Add the finely chopped onion and sprinkle on some vegetable stock, so that it is not too dry, keep cooking for 10' more. Add the cognac and simmer, then add the butter and a drizzle of oil.

Blend everything well, first removing the bay leaf and rosemary. Toast the croutons and place the paté on top, the fig cut into wedges and garnish with a few walnuts.

Serves
4

Difficulty
Low

Time
30'

Game
Deer

Calories
390 Kcal

Chef
Villi Tosi

Wine
Brindisi DOC Negroamaro

Ingredients

G 200 Paua (Abalone) mince
G 150 venison mince
25 wonton wrappers
G 15 fresh chilli
G 5 lemon zest
G 15 spring onions
1 egg yolk
mL 50 extra virgin olive oil
mL 500 sunflower oil
Sweet chilli sauce to taste
Salt and pepper to taste

VENISON AND PAUA WONTONS

Preparation

Combine the Paua and venison meat, the finely sliced chilli, the lemon zest, the finely sliced spring onions and the extra virgin olive oil into a bowl, then mix together. Add salt and pepper.

Lay out wonton wrappers and brush edges with egg yolk.

Take a small amount of the mixture and roll it into a ball. Place this small ball into the center of the wonton wrapper. Fold the wrapper and crimp the edges together. Make sure all edges are firmly pressed together around the ball mixture.

Add the sunflower oil to a fryer, deep dish pan or pot. The oil needs to be at a temperature where the wonton sizzles as soon as you drop them in. A good tip is to break away a small piece of the wonton paper and drop this in. If it sizzles, then the oil is ready, if it doesn't then wait for the piece to sizzle.

By using a long-handled spoon, carefully drop the wontons into the oil. Be careful of the hot oil. Watch the wontons and flip them over multiple times until they are golden and crisp. Remove with the spoon and place on a plate with a paper towel and let the wontons drain the oil away.

Serve with sweet chilli dipping sauce and enjoy.

Serves
4

Difficulty
Low

Time
20'

Game
Duck

Calories
375 Kcal

Chef
Michael Hunter

Wine
Colli Piacentini DOC
Pinot Nero Spumante

DUCK HEART
YAKITORI

Preparation

Start the sauce by adding soy sauce, mirin, sake, rice malt, orange and lemon juice, and sugar to a medium size pot. On high heat, boil to reduce by half. The sauce can be made in advance and chilled and stored in the fridge.

Soak the wood skewers in water over night to prevent burning. Light charcoal at least 15' before grilling.

Cut the green onion into 2.5 cm pieces. Skewer the hearts with a piece of green onion in between each heart (3 per skewer).

Grill the skewers on over the red ambers while brushing the sauce on. The sauce will glaze and stick to the hearts while grilling. After 2-3' flip the hearts and continue brushing the sauce.

The yakitori should have deep char marks from the grill. Cook the other side for 2-3' and serve.

Garnish with chopped green onion and drizzle with the yakitori sauce. The hearts should be served medium rare.

Ingredients

G 450 duck hearts
mL 60 soy sauce
mL 60 mirin
mL 60 sake
mL 60 rice malt (koji)
G 60 granulated sugar
1 orange (juice)
1 lemon (juice)
2 bunches of green onion

Serves
4

Difficulty
Low

Time
30'

Game
Goose

Calories
442 Kcal

Chef
Wade Truong

Wine
Monferrato DOC Rosso

GOOSE BREAST WITH THAI BASIL

Preparation

Clean the goose breasts removing the connective tissue and cut into slices of about ½ centimeter thick.

Mix the soy sauce, black pepper and oil. Pour over the sliced goose breasts and mix to evenly coat. Cover and let it flavor for 30'.

Preheat a wok or wide heavy bottomed saute pan over high heat.

Mix 2 tablespoons of water and cornstarch to make a mixture, set aside.

When the pan is heated, add a thin layer of oil to the pan, then the goose breasts. Allow to cook for about 1', stirring the meat to evenly brown.

Add sliced tomatoes, previously washed, and cook for 30''.

Carefully pour in about half a cup of water and stir, cook for another 30''.

Add in the water and cornstarch mixture and stir to thicken liquids in the pan.

Add in thai basil. Remove from heat, serve immediately.

Ingredients

2 goose breasts
mL 15 soy sauce
G 9 black fresh pepper
mL 15 extra vergin olive oil
G 20 cornstarch
mL 120 water
G 300 tomatoes
G 5 thai basil leaves

Serves
4

Difficulty
Low

Time
50'

Game
Roe deer

Calories
314 Kcal

Chef
Stefano Marinucci

Wine
Morellino di Scansano DOCG

GRILLED VENISON LOIN WITH TOMATO SOUP

Ingredients

G 500 venison loin
G 300 peeled tomatoes
G 200 stale homemade bread
G 100 ribbed tomatoes
1 clove of garlic
Basil to taste
Mixed vegetables for vegetable stock to taste
Salt and pepper to taste
Extra virgin olive oil to taste

Preparation

Season the loin with oil, salt, and pepper and leave to flavor for 10'. Sear the meat on the grill, not too aggressive, being careful not to burn it (about 50° C – 122° F). Remove it and let it rest on a grill to allow the meat to drain.

To prepare the tomato soup, make a vegetable stock that will be used to wet the bread, boiling the vegetables in water for 30'.

Brown the garlic in a large pan with a drizzle of oil and basil, dip the peeled tomatoes and cook for 10', add the homemade bread cut into coarse pieces.

Sprinkle continuously with the stock, until the bread dissolves in the tomato and is well blended. Season with salt and oil.

Compose the plate with the help of a steel ring. Arrange the tomato soup on a serving dish, then the loin of venison cut into slices, finally the ribbed tomato cut into thin slices, garnish with an emulsion of oil, salt, and pepper.

Serves
4

Difficulty
Low

Time
30'

Game
Turkey

Calories
332 Kcal

Chef
Wade Truong

Wine
Bianchello del Metauro
DOC Superiore

Ingredients

G 250 ground turkey meat
3 minced cloves garlic
3 sliced scallions
mL 15 soy sauce
mL 5 sesame oil
G 5 sugar
G 5 black pepper

For breading

3 eggs
G 65 flour
24 shiso leaves or mallow leaves
mL 150 seed oil

For sauce

mL 60 soy sauce
mL 30 white vinegar
G 5 red pepper flake
1 sliced scallion
G 28 sesame seeds

TURKEY STUFFED FRIED SHISO LEAVES

Preparation

Prepare the sauce by mixing the ingredients in a bowl and let stand. At this time, make sure your shiso leaves are lightly damp but not soaking wet, so the flour will adhere to them.

Next, combine all the filling ingredients in a large bowl, mixing well.

Pour flour in a shallow plate. Beat eggs well and pour them through a fine mesh strainer. Reserve the thin egg wash that results, discard the egg that remains in the strainer.

Dip the shiso leaves in the flour on both sides and shake to drop the excess. Place about a tablespoon of meat filling on one side of the leaf and fold it over on itself. Press lightly to flatten it and distribute the meat evenly. Set the folded leaf aside on a dry cutting board or on a sheet pan. Repeat the process with all the leaves.

Preheat the seed oil for frying over medium-high heat.

When the oil is hot, right before frying, dip the stuffed leaves into the strained egg mixture, coating evenly. Shake off excess and fry in oil. Cook for about 1' per side.

Serve immediately with the dipping sauce.

Serves
4

Difficulty
Low

Time
15'

Game
Chamois

Calories
166 Kcal

Chef
Iris Rossi

Wine
Cerasuolo d'Abruzzo DOC

RAW CHAMOIS WITH CITRUS FRUITS

Ingredients

G 400 chamois loin or fillet
G 200 fennel
1 orange
Salt and pepper to taste
Extra virgin olive oil to taste

Preparation

Cut the meat into thin slices, place a slice between two sheets of parchment paper with a little oil and pound with the help of a meat tenderizer, not too forcefully. You will need to do this ensure that the meat thins without breaking.

Remove slice from the parchment paper and place it on the serving dish, repeating with the rest of the slices.

Clean the fennel and remove the hardest parts. Cut it with the help of a slicer into very thin slices and soak them in water with ice.

Remove the orange peel and pith with the aid of a serrated knife, cut the bare segments and divide them into 4 small pieces.

Season the salad and place it at the centre of the plate. Season the carpaccio with salt, pepper, oil and serve.

Serves
4

Difficulty
Medium

Time
50'

Game
Hare

Calories
480 Kcal

Chef
Gabriel Jonsson

Wine
Grignolino d'Asti DOC

HERB-BAKED HARE WITH SWEDISH TURNIP PUREE

Ingredients

G 400 hare saddle
5 Swedish turnips (G 360)
1 jar rosemary
G 30 panko
10 Brussels sprouts
1 savoy cabbage
1 purple cabbage
2 shallots
G 80 butter
mL 400 red wine
4 sprigs of thyme
G 30 beetroot
L 3 meat stock
Salt and pepper to taste
Extra virgin olive oil to taste

Preparation

Peel and chop the turnip into smaller pieces. Boil well-salted water and cook the turnip until soft. Pour off the water but save a few deciliters to use to dilute the puree to the desired size. Pour the turnip into a blender and mix to a smooth cream. Add the butter and boiling water to the desired consistency. Season with salt and pepper.

For the red wine sauce, fry the shallots in butter (G 20) until colored. Add wine, thyme, and beetroot. Let reduce by half. Add the stock and reduce over low heat by half. Strain the sauce, season with salt and pepper and finish by adding 1 tablespoon of butter just before serving.

Set the oven to 150° C (302° F). Salt and pepper the meat, brown the meat all around. Place it on an ovenproof dish and put it in the oven until an internal temperature of 55° C (131° F) and let it rest for about 5' before serving.

For the salad, cut all the cabbages into smaller pieces. Chop the onion. Start by frying the Brussels sprouts in oil until colored. Add the onion and the rest of the cabbage previously hulled and cut into julienne strips.

Serve on a serving dish placing the sauce and meat on one side, the salad and puree on the other side.

Add the chopped parsley and panko to the meat.

Serves
4

Difficulty
Medium

Time
1h 10'

Game
Turkey

Calories
233 Kcal

Chef
Wade Troung

Wine
San Severo DOC Rosato

Ingredients

G 300 turkey
G 150 pork fat
G 75 carrot
G 75 onion
G 30 green onion
G 15 ginger
mL 5 soy sauce
G 7 salt
G 12 black pepper
8 sheets for roulade
Sambal sweet and sour sauce to taste

WILD TURKEY LUMPIA

Preparation

Combine the turkey meat, the pork fat, the carrot, the onion, the green onion, the ginger, the soy sauce, the salt, and pepper, mix well and grind finely using a meat grinder.

Refrigerate for about 30' to firm up the mixture. Place 1 and a half tablespoons of the mixture on the sheet per roulade and roll up. Fry at 175-190° C (350-375° F) for 3' until golden brown and internal temperature is at least 63° C (145° F).

Let drain on a wire rack or plate with paper towels. Serve with the sweet and sour sauce.

Serves
4

Difficulty
Low

Time
45'

Game
Wild boar

Calories
454 Kcal

Chef
Iris Rossi

Wine
Rosso di Montalcino DOC

WILD BOAR CROQUETTE

Ingredients

G 400 wild boar meat
G 200 grated stale bread
G 80 grated parmesan cheese
4 eggs
1 red onion
2 carrots
2 celery legs
mL 250 vegetable stock
mL 150 sunflower oil
Mustard to taste
Salt and pepper to taste
Extra virgin olive oil to taste

Preparation

Sauté the diced celery, carrot, onion, and extra virgin olive oil over low heat. Add the diced pulp and cook it, adding stock as needed.

Let it cool, pass it through a meat grinder and let it rest in a bowl for 5'. Add the parmesan cheese, 2 eggs, a pinch of pepper and a pinch of salt. Mix well and create small balls of about 2 cm.

Place the remaining eggs in a bowl and beat them. Dip the balls first in the egg and then in the breadcrumbs and repeat the process.

Fry the croquettes in boiled sunflower oil and serve warm with a bit of mustard.

Serves
4

Difficulty
Low

Time
40'

Game
Wild boar & roe deer

Calories
214 Kcal

Chef
Iris Rossi

Wine
Chianti Colli Arentini DOCG

CHITARRINE WITH GAME RAGOUT

Ingredients

G 150 minced wild boar meat
G 150 ground venison meat
G 320 chitarrine pasta
G 500 tomato sauce
1 white onion
Juniper berries to taste
Rosemary to taste
Salt and pepper to taste
Extra virgin olive oil to taste

Preparation

Brown the diced onion in a pan with a little oil. Add the wild boar and venison meat.

Brown the meat well, add the tomato sauce and juniper berries. Cook over low heat for about 10-15' and add salt and pepper to taste.

Cook the chitarrine in plenty of salted water, check the cooking time on the package. Drain the pasta and toss for a few minutes with the meat ragout.

Serve the chitarrine with a sprig of fresh rosemary and freshly ground pepper.

Serves
4

Difficulty
Medium

Time
1h 10'

Game
Deer

Calories
667 Kcal

Chef
Iris Rossi

Wine
Valpolicella DOC

Ingredients

G 600 lean venison meat
G 400 type 00 flour
G 400 boiled potatoes
3 eggs
1 white onion
G 20 butter
Rosemary to taste
Salt and pepper to taste
Extra virgin olive oil to taste

WILD GNOCCO
WITH VENISON RAGOUT

Preparation

Pour the flour and potatoes, previously mashed in a potato masher, into a bowl and form a hollow. Pour the eggs in the center and knead by hand until you get a homogeneous dough. Form a ball, wrap it in plastic wrap and let it rest in the refrigerator for at least 30'.

Mash the dough a bit and cut it, dividing it into equal parts. Form long ropes with the dough about 1 cm wide and cut them into square pieces. Roll them out in a tray with a little flour to prevent them from sticking.

Brown the diced onion in a pan with a little oil. Add the ground venison meat and brown it. Add 1 glass of water and the butter. Cook over low heat for about 10-15'.

Cook the gnocchi in salted boiling water, drain them and place them in the pan with the meat sauce as soon as they rise to the surface.

Sauté for a few minutes and serve with two leaves of fresh rosemary.

Serves
4

Difficulty
Medium

Time
50'

Game
Roe deer

Calories
518 Kcal

Chef
Stefano Marinucci

Wine
Cirò DOC Rosato

COLD CALAMARATA WITH VENISON LOIN TARTARE

Ingredients

G 400 venison loin
G 300 calamarata pasta
G 100 parsley
G 80 honey pecorino cheese
G 180 yellow cherry tomatoes
1 lime
Mashed oats to taste
Red turnip sprouts to taste
Salt and pepper to taste
Extra virgin olive oil to taste

Preparation

Cook the pasta in salted boiling water, drain it while still "al dente" and cool it down.

Prepare the loin of venison, removing the outer skin, and make sure you have cut it down for at least 48 h.

Cut the meat finely with a knife, season with extra virgin olive oil, salt, pepper and lime juice.

Blend the parsley with a spoonful of cold water, oil, salt and pepper.

Fry the yellow tomatoes, stewing them first with a little water and then with a drizzle of oil and a pinch of salt.

Prepare the dish by placing the pasta first, then the venison tartare, the cherry tomatoes and finally the parsley pesto. Decorate the dish with a sprinkling of pecorino cheese, the sprouts, and the oats for decoration.

Finish with a drizzle of oil and a sprinkle of pepper.

Serves
4

Difficulty
Medium

Time
40'

Game
Wild boar

Calories
831 Kcal

Chef
Iris Rossi

Wine
Verdicchio di Matelica Riserva DOCG

ACORN TAGLIATELLE AND WILD BOAR BACON

Ingredients

G 200 wild boar bacon
G 300 acorn flour
G 400 fresh broad bean
G 100 cherry tomatoes confit
3 eggs
1 white onion
Salt to taste
Extra virgin olive oil to taste

Preparation

Prepare the fresh pasta by forming a circle with the flour and place the eggs in the center, add a pinch of salt and continue to knead until you get an elastic and smooth dough. Form a ball, wrap it in plastic wrap and let it rest in the refrigerator for at least 30'.

Roll out the ball forming a thin sheet with a little flour. Cut the dough into tagliatelle (0.7 cm thick).

Pour the oil into a frying pan over low heat. Add the onion, previously cut into julienne strips. As soon as the onion begins to brown, add the fresh fava beans, and cook for about 10', adding a little water.

In another pan, brown the bacon until crispy.

Add the bacon to the broad beans and toss in the tagliatelle previously cooked in salted boiling water. Place in a serving dish.

Serves
4

Difficulty
Low

Time
25'

Game
Wild boar

Calories
518 Kcal

Chef
Michael Hunter

Wine
Cesanese del Piglio DOCG

WILD BOAR SPAGHETTI CARBONARA

Ingredients

G 450 wild boar bacon and pancetta
G 450 spaghetti pasta
G 75 grated parmesan cheese
G 75 grated pecorino cheese
3 eggs
3 egg yolks
1 minced small shallot
2 sliced green onions
2 minced cloves garlic
G 6 cracked black pepper
Salt to taste

Preparation

Cut the wild boar bacon into 1-2 cm cubes and sauté in a skillet over high heat. Cook until the edges are golden brown but not completely crispy.

Add the shallot and garlic, sauté for another 2' and turn off. Cook the pasta in salted boiling water and drain it while still "al dente". Reserve 240 ml of the cooking water.

Mix the eggs and yolks with a pinch of salt and the pepper and half of the cheese. Add the pasta water to the pan with the pasta and turn on low heat. When ¾ of the water has evaporated, turn off the heat and add the beaten eggs, stir, or toss together with the bacon.

Add the rest of the cheese and continue to stir.

Distribute on plates, grate more parmesan cheese and garnish with sliced green onions.

Serves
4

Difficulty
Medium

Time
3h

Game
Deer

Calories
800 Kcal

Chef
Michael Hunter

Wine
Vino Nobile
di Montepulciano DOCG

Ingredients

Kg 1.5 deboned venison meat
1 large spanish onion
1 carrot
2 stalks celery
6 tomatoes
G 150 wild mushrooms
4 cloves garlic
mL 200 red wine
L 1.5 dark venison stock
mL 100 extra virgin olive oil
G 650 Cavatelli dumplings
(gnocchi can be substituted)
G 200 diced butternut squash
G 200 diced turnip
G 200 diced parsnip
6 leaves of kale
G 200 grated parmesan cheese
G 50 unsalted butter
1 bouquet garnish (thyme, parsley, and bay leaves tied with twine)
Pinch of chilli flakes to taste
Salt and pepper to taste

VENISON RAGOUT
CAVATELLI PASTA

Preparation

Preheat a large cast iron skillet or pot.

Cut the vegetables into medium dices, slice the mushrooms into large pieces, crush and mince garlic. Tie the herbs with string.

Season venison meat generously with salt and pepper. Add oil to the hot pan and add the venison meat to the pan; do not stir or flip until the meat is caramelized, 3-4′ per side.

Transfer to a roasting pan, then add the vegetables to the pan, sauté to caramelize. Add the minced garlic and stir, deglaze with red wine.

Transfer the wine and vegetables to the roasting pan, add the stock and herbs, mushrooms and cover with foil.

Bake 162° C (325° F) for 2 h 30' or until meat is tender and pick with fork into large pieces, leaving in the liquid to cool.

Fill one pot with salted water and bring to the boil. Small dice root vegetables, tear kale off stem and roughly chop.

Heat a second pot and sauté the vegetables until tender in butter and extra virgin olive oil. Add the braising liquid, pulled venison meat, reduce.

Cook fresh Cavatelli in boiling water for 5′. Transfer Cavatelli to ragout, stirring with your wooden spoon, add cheese and cook for an additional 2′.

Spoon into your serving bowls and top with more grated parmesan.

Serves
4

Difficulty
Medium

Time
40'

Game
Partridge

Calories
671 Kcal

Chef
Stefano Marinucci

Wine
Lugana Superiore DOC

PARTRIDGE FARFALLE WITH CHEESE AND PEPPER CREAM

Ingredients

G 250 partridge breasts
G 50 leek
G 150 Casatella Trevigiana DOP cheese
G 100 parmesan cheese
1 garlic clove
mL 100 dry white wine
3 eggs
G 300 re-milled whole flour
Bay leaves to taste
Apple cider vinegar to taste
Fresh sorrel leaves to taste
Sweet paprika to taste
Salt and pepper to taste
Extra virgin olive oil taste

For the sauce

mL 50 cold water
G 100 pecorino cheese
G 150 Casatella Trevigiana DOP cheese
Sichuan aromatic pepper to taste
Extra virgin olive oil to taste

Preparation

Clean the breasts by removing the outer skin and cut them into cubes, put them in a pan and brown the meat, add the finely chopped leek, add oil, salt and pepper. After about 3-4', add a little vinegar and let it evaporate.

Deglaze with white wine, add crushed garlic and bay leaf, cover and leave for 5'. When it is cooked, pass it through a cutter to blend it well and evenly, then add the parmesan and Casatella Trevigiana cheeses.

Prepare the fresh pasta by forming a circle with the flour and place the eggs in the center, add a pinch of salt and continue to knead until you get an elastic and smooth dough. Let it rest for about 10', then roll out the dough to a thickness of about 4 mm, using a pastry cutter, form 8 cm squares on each side, and fill with partridge breast meat using an amount equal to a walnut kernel.

Close the dough starting with the flap; if you like, you can moisten the edges slightly so that the closure stays tighter.

For the sauce, whisk the cheeses, oil, pepper and a little cold water. Pour everything into the saucepan where you cooked the partridge, leaving for a few minutes.

Cook the stuffed farfalle in previously salted boiling water and drain after 3-4', place on a plate along with the sauce and a sprinkling of sweet paprika, finishing with a drizzle of oil and a grind of pepper. Garnish with sorrel leaves.

Serves
4

Difficulty
Medium

Time
40'

Game
Wild boar

Calories
553 Kcal

Chef
Michael Hunter

Wine
Nizza DOCG

Ingredients

G 500 wild boar loin
G 200 white onion
mL 100 whole milk
G 10 potato starch
G 100 Grana Padano cheese
G 50 Piedmont hazelnuts
Parsley to taste
Carrots and celery to taste
Laurel to taste
Meat stock to taste
Salt and pepper to taste
Extra virgin olive oil to taste

For the pasta

G 250 semolina
G 95 beetroot
mL 15 water
Sugar to taste

RED TAGLIATELLE WITH WILD BOAR AND HAZELNUT RAGOUT

Preparation

Wash the wild boar loin well, clean it. Cut the meat into small pieces, put it in a saucepan, blanch it and, after a few minutes, add the oil, half the finely chopped onion, salt and pepper. After about 8', add some stock and cook for about 30' with the lid on.

Clean the beetroots from any stems and wash them well. Put them in a pan and cover them with cold water. Add a little salt and a pinch of sugar and boil everything over low heat for 45'.

Once cooked, pass the beets under cold water for a moment, remove the peel, cut them into slices and blend them. Let it cool. You can also cook the beets the day before.

Prepare the fresh pasta by forming a circle with the semolina and introduce the beets and water in the center, add a pinch of salt and continue to knead until you obtain an elastic and smooth dough.

Let it rest for 10', then roll out the dough to about 4 mm thick and cut the tagliatelle.

For the onion cream, simmer the milk with the remaining finely chopped onions and the cheese, add a pinch of salt and the starch diluted in a little water.

Cook the tagliatelle in a salted boiling water, drain them as soon as they rise to the surface, toss them in the wild boar ragout and finish the dish with a drizzle of oil, a sprinkle of pepper and the Chioggia onion cream.

Serves
4

Difficulty
Medium

Time
1h 30'

Game
Wild boar

Calories
447 Kcal

Chef
Roberto Dormicchi

Wine
Lambrusco Mantovano DOC

WILD BOAR TORTELLO AND AUTUMN SCENT

Ingredients

G 200 wild boar lean meat
G 20 onion
1 clove of garlic
1 sprig of rosemary
1 small cup of white wine
G 30 grated parmesan cheese
1 egg yolk
3 eggs
G 260 flour
Sage, marjoram, thyme to taste
Salt to taste
Extra virgin olive oil to taste

For the broth

1 sprig of rosemary
Wild berries infusion to taste
Orange zest to taste

Preparation

Mix the flour and eggs, adding a pinch of salt and let the dough rest, cover it with a cling film in the refrigerator for 10'.

Roll out the dough and cut into disks with a pastry cutter.

Prepare a sauté with the extra virgin olive oil, the onion into brunoise, the crushed garlic, then add the meat cut into regular cubes and the aromatic herbs.

Cook the meat, pour in the wine, let it evaporate, then season with salt and pepper.

Pass the meat through the mincer twice, add the parmesan cheese, the egg yolk and mix. Stuff the pasta discs and close them to make a tortello.

Infuse the berries with the orange peel and rosemary, filter, bring to a boil, and season with salt.

Cook the tortelli in salted water, drain, then arrange in a serving dish, with grated orange peel in the microplane, flowers, sprig of rosemary, and the berries infusion.

Serves
4

Difficulty
Medium

Time
45'

Game
Wild boar

Calories
615 Kcal

Chef
Michael Hunter

Wine
Colli Bolognesi DOC
Bologna Rosso

WILD BOAR BOLOGNESE

Ingredients

G 450 ground wild boar
G 400 conchiglie pasta
mL 30 extra virgin olive oil
G 15 kosher salt
G 10 black pepper
G 250 diced white onion
G 125 diced carrot
G 125 diced celery
G 60 minced garlic
mL 500 dark stock
mL 250 dry white wine
G 500 tomato sauce
G 30 tomato paste
3 bay leaves
2 sprigs fresh thyme
Red chilli flakes to taste
Parmesan cheese to taste
Basil to taste

Preparation

Heat a large, heavy pot over high heat. Add the olive oil, ground wild boar, salt, pepper and cook, stirring with a wooden spoon, until the meat is browned.

Add the onion, carrot, celery, garlic, and chilli flakes and cook, stirring occasionally, for 2'.

Add white wine, the stock, tomatoes and their juice, tomato paste, bay leaves, and thyme.

Reduce the heat to medium-low and simmer, uncovered, until the sauce has thickened, about 30-40'.

Remove from the heat, discard the bay leaves and thyme stems, and keep warm while you cook the pasta.

Cook the pasta to your desired doneness drain the water and toss with the sauce to combine.

Serve hot, garnishing with chopped basil and freshly grated parmesan cheese.

Serves
4

Difficulty
Low

Time
40'

Game
Roe deer

Calories
367 Kcal

Chef
Roberto Dormicchi

Wine
Offida Pecorino DOCG

POLENTA
ROSEMARY AND VENISON

Ingredients

G 150 venison chunks
G 150 polenta
mL 500 vegetable stock
G 100 pre-cooked chickpeas
1 clove of garlic
Rosemary to taste
Salt and black pepper to taste
Extra virgin olive oil to taste

Preparation

Let boil the vegetable stock, then season with the salt and gradually add the corn flour, stirring constantly with a whisk. Cook for about 15'.

Toss the pre-cooked chickpeas with rosemary, extra virgin olive oil, salt and pepper.

Toss the venison chunks in a non-stick pan with garlic and extra virgin olive oil.

Add it to the polenta. Pour the soft polenta into a serving dish and garnish with rosemary. Serve hot.

Serves
4

Difficulty
Medium

Time
40'

Game
Moose

Calories
367 Kcal

Chef
Gabriel Jonsson

Wine
Dogliani DOCG

NOODLE SALAD WITH MOOSE

Ingredients

G 600 moose meat
G 300 rice noodles
10 sugar snaps
G 45 sliced kale
10 cherry tomatoes
8 asparagus
½ silver onion
½ fennel
Salt and pepper to taste
Extra virgin olive oil to taste

For dressing

2 lime (juice)
mL 45 fish sauce
mL 15 rice vinegar
mL 15 soy sauce
mL 20 sesame oil
5 drops of Worcester sauce
1 chopped clove of garlic
G 15 sugar
G 15 chopped red chilli

Preparation

Mix lime juice, fish sauce, rice vinegar, soy sauce, sesame oil, Worcester sauce, garlic, sugar, and chilli, and let it stand for a while.

Boil the rice noodles according to the instructions on the package.

Cut the vegetables into strips or desired sizes. Mix the vegetables with the dressing.

Salt and pepper the meat. Fry in oil to an internal temperature of 48° C (119° F) and let the meat rest for about 5-10′. Then it should reach a temperature of about 55° C (131° F) (medium).

Mix the dressing with the noodles and put it on a plate. Cut the meat and top the noodles with it.

Serves
4

Difficulty
Low

Time
40'

Game
Wild boar

Calories
710 Kcal

Chef
Roberto Dormicchi

Wine
Etna DOC Rosato

MINESTRONE SOUP WITH WILD BOAR SAUSAGE AND BACON

Preparation

Heat the extra virgin olive oil in a pan, add the chopped shallot and then all the vegetables except spinach and tomatoes. Cook for 10'.

Add the tomatoes and the spinach, season with salt and pepper.

Roast the sausages cut into cubes and the bacon (both sides) into a non-stick frying pan.

Place the minestrone soup with the roasted sausage and bacon on a serving dish.

Garnish with dried black truffle to ensure crunchiness.

Ingredients

G 300 fresh wild boar sausages
G 100 wild boar bacon
G 30 chopped shallot
G 50 diced carrots
G 50 diced celery
G 30 diced ripe tomatoes
G 50 washed spinach
G 30 frozen peas
G 50 diced potatoes
G 20 dried black truffle
Salt and pepper to taste
Extra virgin olive oil to taste

Serves
4

Difficulty
Low

Time
30'

Game
Pheasant

Calories
285 Kcal

Chef
Roberto Dormicchi

Wine
Rosso Piceno DOC

Ingredients

G 200 pheasant breasts
G 400 pappardelle pasta
G 100 ground mixed meat
mL 80 extra virgin olive oil
G 250 tomato sauce
G 50 taggiasca olives
1 anchovy
G 30 diced onion
G 30 diced celery
G 30 diced carrot
1 clove of garlic
Salt and pepper to taste

PAPPARDELLE WITH PHEASANT SAUCE

Preparation

Prepare a sauté with oil, celery, carrot, onion, garlic, anchovy, and taggiasca olives.

Take care that the anchovy melts while the sauté is browning.

Combine the ground mixed meat, the breasts of pheasant and browned. Separate the pieces of meat with a wooden spoon. Add the tomato sauce and cook for about 15'.

Cook the pappardelle in salted boiling water. Drain the pappardelle "al dente" and sautéed into sauce of pheasant.

Serves
4

Difficulty
Medium

Time
40'

Game
Snipe

Calories
606 Kcal

Chef
Stefano Marinucci

Wine
Valcalepio Rosso DOC

BALDO RICE WITH SNIPE

Ingredients

4 snipes
G 320 Baldo rice
1 white onion
2 carrots
2 celery ribs
6 radishes
mL 100 milk
G 300 Casatella Trevigiana DOP cheese
G 50 butter
mL 300 white wine
2 slices of bacon
G 20 chestnut honey
Fresh mint to taste
Salt and pepper to taste
Extra virgin olive oil to taste

Preparation

Wash the snipes under running water and flame off any remaining feathers. Cut the snipes in two halves, vertically. Leave one half whole with the entire head, while the other will be boned leaving the breasts whole. Once the breasts have been removed, cut the remaining meat with a knife.

Prepare a stock that will be used for cooking the risotto, with the snipe bones, celery, carrots, and onion, after having washed and diced them. Toast the pieces of meat in a pan with half an onion and a drizzle of oil for a few minutes.

Add the Baldo rice, toast it and deglaze it with white wine, then add two peeled radishes. Continue to cook, stirring constantly and pouring in the stock as the rice absorbs it.

Season the other half of the snipes with salt and pepper, cook them for 10′ on each side in a pan with a drizzle of oil, garlic, salt, pepper and the chopped bacon, add a ladle of stock, drizzle with honey and bake for about 20′ at 160° C (320° F). When they are browned and crispy, remove them from the oven and use them for the final composition of the dish.

Heat the chopped Casatella Trevigiana cheese in a small pan, leaving some aside for the final garnish, and the butter, without bringing them to the boil (about 70° C – 158° F), then pour the cream into the rice.

When cooked, plate the risotto, lay the halves of the snipes on top, garnish with a drizzle of oil, a few thin slices of radish, fresh mint and a sprinkling of Casatella Trevigiana cheese.

Serves
4

Difficulty
Low

Time
30'

Game
Partridge

Calories
560 Kcal

Chef
Roberto Dormicchi

Wine
Verdicchio dei Castelli
di Jesi DOC Spumante

RISOTTO STRAWBERRIES AND PARTRIDGES

Ingredients

G 300 knife-pounded partridge meat
G 300 Carnaroli rice
G 50 butter
G 80 grated parmesan cheese
G 160 fresh strawberries
1 lime
Vegetable stock to taste
Ginger to taste
Salt and pepper to taste

Preparation

Toast the rice in butter and continue cooking adding gradually hot stock.

Cook the meat over high heat in a non-stick frying pan. At 5′ from the end of cooking add the meat to the rice, and stir well with parmesan, some ginger and grated lime zest. Add salt to taste.

Garnish with strawberry slices and fresh ground black pepper. Serve hot.

Serves
4

Difficulty
Medium

Time
1h 15'

Game
Deer

Calories
443 Kcal

Chef
Villi Tosi

Wine
Suvereto Merlot DOCG

Ingredients

4 venison back steaks
½ potato
½ orange kumara
G 250 frozen peas
G 7.5 turmeric
G 20 butter
mL 10 milk
G 5 salt
G 5 pepper
Nutmeg to taste
Extra virgin olive oil to taste

For the berry sauce

G 380 berries
mL 115 balsamic vinegar
G 150 white sugar
mL 60 apple cider vinegar
1 lemon
3 cloves
2 star anise
Rosemary or thyme to taste

VENISON BACK STEAK
WITH BERRY SAUCE

Preparation

Peel the potato and the orange, cut them into small cubes and put them in a pot. Cover with water, add a pinch of salt and bring to a boil. Cook until soft to the fork.

Add a knob of butter and a drop of milk and mash the potato to make a smooth puree.

Preheat the oven to 180° C (356° F). Dry the surface of the meat with paper towels and make sure all tendons have been removed. Combine salt, pepper and nutmeg in a small bowl. Sprinkle the mix all over the meat.

Sauté the oil in a pan over high heat. Once hot, sear the meat, turning every 30'' or so to make sure all sides are browned. Then place in a baking dish and bake in the oven for 4-5'. Remove from oven, place on a cutting board and let rest for 5-10' before slicing. It should be pink in the center.

Boil the peas for 1'. Drain them and place them in an extractor or immersion blender.

Add a knob of butter and a drop of milk. Blend gently, but not into a puree. You will only need to blend the peas once or twice.

For the sauce, combine the berries, sugar, vinegar, lemon zest and juice, cloves and star anise in a pan, and bring to a boil. Add a pinch of salt, if you like. After about 5', you should be able to mash the berries on the side of the saucepan using a wooden spoon. Continue to quickly simmer the sauce another 5-10' to thicken it.

Place the mashed potatoes in the center and lay the meat on top. Add some peas on the side and the berry sauce on top of the meat. Finish by adjusting the salt and pepper and a sprig of rosemary or thyme on the side.

Serves
4

Difficulty
Low

Time
2h 30'

Game
Pheasant

Calories
630 Kcal

Chef
Michael Hunter

Wine
Alto Adige Cabernet
Sauvignon DOC

PHEASANT AU VIN
WITH SPÄTZLE

Ingredients

2 whole pheasants (approx. 2.75 kg)
G 225 sliced bacon (1 cm)
G 250 whole pearl onions
G 500 cremini mushrooms
L 1 game bird stock
mL 500 red wine
G 155 tomato paste
G 200 green beans
4 bay leaves
1 sprig of rosemary
2 sprigs of thyme
1 clove of garlic
G 500 all-purpose flour
mL 125 whole milk
4 whole eggs
1 pinch of ground nutmeg
1 pinch of pepper
G 5 salt
G 5 thyme
G 15 grain mustard
Parsley to taste
Salt and pepper to taste
Extra virgin olive oil to taste

Preparation

Cut the pheasant in half along the back. Divide the breasts in half and separate the thighs, so you get 6 pieces per pheasant. Season the meat with salt and pepper. Preheat a large pan over high heat.

Add the bacon and cook until crispy, 4-5' over medium heat, remove from heat and reserve.

Add pheasant with skin side down and cook 2-3' per side, until golden brown. Remove the meat from the pan and add the onions, mushrooms, previously cleaned and halved, and crispy bacon. Cook for 2-3'.

Add the pheasant again and then the wine. Cook off the alcohol for 2-3', add the stock and tomato paste. Cover and transfer to oven at 160° C (320° F) and cook for about 2 h 30'.

Clean the green beans and cook them in a pan, with a mixture of oil and garlic, for 15-20'. Add salt and pepper to taste.

Place the flour, milk, eggs, nutmeg, salt, pepper, thyme and mustard in a mixing bowl. Whisk on medium speed for 4-5'.

Bring the salted water to a boil, cut the pasta into strips with a spatula, directly into the boiling water. Drain the pasta as soon as it rises to the surface.

Stir-fry the Spätzle over a high heat in a little oil and butter and arrange them, slightly crispy, on the serving plate.

Arrange the pheasant on Spätzle (or mashed potatoes or rice) with the green beans, mushrooms and onion.

Serves
4

Difficulty
Medium

Time
1h 30'

Game
Reindeer

Calories
719 Kcal

Chef
Gabriel Jonsson

Wine
Carignano del Sulcis DOC

REINDEER FILLET WITH POTATO CAKE

Ingredients

G 600 reindeer fillet
G 50 butter for the meat
4 leaves of kale
12 cherry tomatoes
3 shallots
mL 15 Champagne vinegar
6 potatoes
G 70 grated priest cheese
1 yellow onion
2 cloves of garlic
G 200 butter for the cake
mL 400 red wine
1 small piece of beetroot
mL 300 game stock
G 28 butter for the wine sauce
8 junipers
5 sprigs of thyme
2 sprigs of rosemary
Salt and pepper to taste
Extra virgin olive oil to taste

Preparation

Trim the meat removing the nervous parts and keep them for the sauce. Chop the shallot and brown it together with the meat scraps.

Lightly crush the juniper berries, add them along with the wine, 4 sprigs of thyme, 1 of rosemary, beetroot, and beet. Cook over low heat until the sauce is reduced by half. Add the stock and let it reduce further. Strain everything and season with salt and pepper. Add a knob of butter just before serving.

Prepare the potato cake by combining the butter with the thinly sliced onion and crushed garlic. Melt the butter with rosemary and thyme. Peel and slice the potatoes very thinly with a mandoline.

Brush a baking dish with melted butter and place a layer of potatoes, brush the potatoes with butter and sprinkle with a little cheese. Also make an even layer with the onion, previously cut up. Continue making layers until the cake is about 3 cm thick. Finish with a layer of potatoes and butter.

Bake in the oven at 220° C (428° F) for about 35'. Let rest in the refrigerator before reheating and serving.

Prepare a salad by dicing the cabbage, tomatoes and onion finely. Dress with vinegar, oil, salt and pepper.

Season the meat with salt and pepper. Heat the oil in a pan, brown the meat on both sides. Lower the heat and add the butter and herbs. Sauté the meat and cook over high heat until it reaches an internal temperature of 50° C (122° F). Remove the meat and let it rest at least 5' before serving. Serve with plenty of sauce.

Serves
4

Difficulty
Medium

Time
1h 30'

Game
Fallow deer

Calories
319 Kcal

Chef
Stefano Marinucci

Wine
Barbera d'Alba DOC

Ingredients

G 800 venison fillet
G 200 wild rice
G 200 purple cabbage
G 100 leek
1 red onion (about G 100)
G 5 starch
Beetroot sprouts to taste
Sesame seeds to taste
Vegetable stock to taste
Soy sauce to taste
Salt and pepper to taste
Extra virgin olive oil to taste

VENISON FILLET WITH SESAME, WILD RICE AND PURPLE CABBAGE

Preparation

Clean the venison fillet well, dry it, season with salt, pepper and a drizzle of oil and leave it to flavor for 20'.

Boil the cabbage in water and let it cook for 20', season with salt, add the starch to bind the sauce, pass with an immersion blender until you obtain a blue-purple sauce.

Boil the rice in the vegetable stock for about 40' and drain it al dente, then roll it in the leek leaves.

Divide the fillet into four equal portions, breading them in sesame seeds.

Cook the meat in a very hot pan 2' each side, remove and cover it to keep it warm.

In the same pan add the red onion cut into cloves with a drizzle of oil and salt.

Cut the leek into slices about 1 cm high and blanch in a pan, adding the soy sauce.

Prepare the dish taking care to first place the outer leaf of the leek, then the meat, the onion, the seared leek, finally the sauce with the beetroot sprouts and the leek rolls and wild rice.

To give it a final touch, smoke under a glass dome with olive-scented wood.

Serves
4

Difficulty
Low

Time
60'

Game
Deer

Calories
557 Kcal

Chef
Gabriel Jonsson

Wine
Colli Pesaresi DOC Rosso

GAMEBURGER

Ingredients

G 400 minced meat
G 150 tallow frozen
G 70 parmesan cheese
4 leaves black cabbage
4 leaves purple cabbage
mL 15 vinegar
mL 15 extra virgin olive oil
G 50 mayonnaise
3 junipers
G 15 onion powder
G 15 dried thyme
½ silver onion
2 tomatoes
4 hamburger buns
Roasted onion to taste
Salt and pepper to taste

Preparation

Mix the mayonnaise with onion powder, thyme and finely chopped juniper berries, taste with salt and pepper.

Start by shredding the cabbages into thin strips and mix with vinegar and extra virgin olive oil, massaging the cabbage well.

Cut the tomatoes into slices and cut the silver onion into very thin, preferably on a mandolin.

Grate the frozen tallow and mix it with the minced meat. Shape into four balls of equal size.

Heat a frying pan on maximum heat and put in the minced meat balls, press customs firmly with a frying pan or something else suitable to make the hamburgers. Salt and pepper.

Fry the meat until it has a nice surface, turn around. Put on the cheese and place a metal bowl over the meat so the cheese melts.

Remove and let the meat rest on the toasted bread.

Top the burger with plenty of mayonnaise, cabbages, onions, tomatoes, and onion powder. Serve it with French fries.

VENISON LOIN
WITH ZABAGLIONE AND CRUNCHY SPINACH

Serves
4

Difficulty
Medium

Time
1h 45'

Game
Roe deer

Calories
495 Kcal

Chef
Roberto Dormicchi

Wine
Montefalco DOC

Ingredients

G 400 venison loin
3 egg yolks
G 50 grated parmesan cheese
mL 100 fresh cream
G 50 butter
mL 100 white wine
G 400 fresh leaf spinach
5 sage leaves
1 sprig of rosemary
1 clove of garlic
Salt and pepper to taste
Extra virgin olive oil to taste

Preparation

Season the loin, previously cured of all the ribs and skin, with rosemary, sage, garlic and put in a vacuum bag with white wine, oil, condition at 99%. Cook at 56° C (133° F) for 60'.

Clean the previously washed spinach by removing the stem, sauté in a hot pan adding salt and butter.

Place the egg yolks in a bowl, place in a bain-marie, beat with parmesan cheese, cream, salt, and pepper.

Remove the meat from the vacuum bag and drain it.

Roast the loin on all sides in a non-sticky pan and season with salt and pepper.

Arrange the escalope loin on a serving dish, accompanied with hot cheese zabaglione and crispy spinach.

Serves
4

Difficulty
Low

Time
15-20'

Game
Deer

Calories
728 Kcal

Chef
Michael Hunter

Wine
Valle d'Aosta DOC Nebbiolo

VENISON BACKSTRAP WITH CREAMY POLENTA

Ingredients

Kg 1 venison backstrap
mL 500 whole milk
G 15 kosher salt
G 125 instant polenta
G 125 parmesan cheese
G 140 butter
G 450 spinach
4 cloves of garlic
Salt and pepper to taste
Extra virgin olive oil to taste

Preparation

Pour milk into a pot and add a pinch of salt. Bring to a boil over medium heat, then whisk in the polenta steadily.

Reduce the heat to low and cook, stirring every 3-5', making sure to scrape the bottom of the pot to prevent burning and sticking, until the polenta has reached the right density, 5-10'.

Remove from heat and stir in freshly grated parmesan cheese and butter. Keep warm. While the polenta is cooking, heat a cast-iron pan over high heat.

Season the venison with salt and pepper and add the oil to the pan. Brown the meat over high heat for 2-3' per side or until golden brown.

Transfer the pan to the 178° C (352° F) oven and bake until the internal temperature reaches 46° C (115° F), for medium rare.

Let the meat rest for 5' before slicing.

Fry the garlic in 15 g of butter and add the spinach previously cleaned and stalk removed.

Wilt them over medium-high heat for 2-3'.

Plate the polenta, spinach and evenly sliced venison.

Serves
4

Difficulty
Low

Time
30'

Game
Goose

Calories
705 Kcal

Chef
Michael Hunter

Wine
Ruchè di Castagnole
Monferrato DOCG

SNOW GOOSE
WITH CHIMICHURRI

Ingredients

4 goose breasts (approx. 1 Kg)
2 bunches of asparagus
G 450 new potatoes (spring baby potatoes)
2 stalks of green onions
Butter to taste
Salt and pepper to taste

For the chimichurri

2 jalapeños
1 bunch of cilantro
mL 230 extra virgin olive oil
mL 30 apple cider vinegar
1 lemon (juice)
1 tbsp of pesto
½ bunch of parsley
4 cloves of garlic
Salt and pepper to taste

Preparation

Mix all the ingredients of the chimichurri recipe together after previously finely chopping the herbs by hand or with a food processor. Allow to season for at least 10' before serving.

In a medium-sized pot, steam the potatoes until soft, then about 15-20', remove the water and add a tablespoon of butter, salt to taste and the chopped spring onions.

Season the goose meat with salt and pepper, drizzle the asparagus with oil and salt.

Grill meat and asparagus over high heat; cook goose for 2-3' per side. Grill asparagus until cooked through.

Let the meat rest for 5' before slicing. Arrange the meat with the asparagus and potatoes and garnish with the chimichurri.

Serves
4

Difficulty
Medium

Time
2h

Game
Wild boar

Calories
341 Kcal

Chef
Stefano Marinucci

Wine
Rosso di Montepulciano DOC

WILD BOAR OSSOBUCO WITH BEER

Ingredients

8 slices of wild boar marrowbone
mL 750 beer
2 white onions
2 cloves of garlic
2 carrots
2 apples
G 60 butter
3 sweet potatoes
Juniper berries to taste
Rosemary to taste
Cloves to taste
Flour to taste
Salt and pepper to taste
Extra virgin olive oil to taste

Preparation

Clean the onions and carrots, leaving aside a little for the stock and a little for the meat. Clean the sweet potatoes, leaving them aside for the side dish.

Put the wild boar marrowbones in a bowl with the beer, apples, carrots, garlic, a pinch of salt, the juniper berries and a sprig of rosemary; leave to flavor overnight.

Prepare a classic stock with carrots and onions, beef bones and cloves, simmer for about 60'.

Drain and flour the meat, place it in a saucepan with oil and butter.

As soon as it is browned, add the onions and carrots cut into cubes, simmer with the beer and continue cooking, adding the meat stock.

Cook the sweet potatoes in the microwave, piercing them with a toothpick and covering them with cling film; let them cook for 10'. Once cooked, make a puree.

Compose the dish, placing the sweet potato puree, some vegetables and the wild boar marrowbones with their sauce at the base.

Serves
4

Difficulty
Medium

Time
2h 30'

Game
Thrush

Calories
312 Kcal

Chef
Stefano Marinucci

Wine
Aglianico del Vulture DOC

THRUSHES WITH POLENTA BEANS AND PEA CREAM

Ingredients

8 thrushes
G 100 fresh peas
G 100 fresh beans like borlotto
1 green onion
4 slices of bacon
G 100 yellow polenta
L 1 vegetable stock
1 clove of garlic
Bay leaf and basil to taste
Apple cider vinegar to taste
Salt to taste
Black and pink pepper to taste
Extra virgin olive oil to taste

Preparation

Prepare the polenta with the traditional method then let it cool, cut it into the desired shape.

Clean the thrushes well by putting them in a saucepan, pluck them, pass them over a flame to eliminate even the shortest feathers, then remove the entrails; wash them under running water and let them dry.

Heat the oil in a pan, add the bay leaf and pink pepper and then add the thrushes, brown on all sides until the meat has browned. Season with salt, add a little hot stock and cook over low heat for 50', wet the meat from time to time with the stock.

Boil the fresh peas in plenty of water for 10', drain and toss in a pan with a spring onion and basil, season with salt and pepper. Simmer them and keep them warm.

After leaving the beans to soak for one night, boil them in plenty of water for 30' and season with oil, salt and pepper.

When the thrushes are almost at the end of cooking, cut the slices of bacon into strips, brown it a little in a pan, then add it to the thrushes, simmer with the apple cider vinegar.

Heat the polenta in a pan with a drizzle of oil. Serve spreading the pea cream on the plate, place the polenta and the thrushes with their sauce on top.

Serves
4

Difficulty
Low

Time
30'

Game
Quail

Calories
391 Kcal

Chef
Stefano Marinucci

Wine
Alto Adige Chardonnay DOC

CLEAR BAG OF QUAIL

Ingredients

4 quails
G 100 carrots
G 100 zucchini
G 50 fresh onion
G 30 yellow tomatoes (approx. 8)
4 pcs of paper cooking film
Parsley to taste
Fennel seeds to taste
Vegetable stock to taste
Salt and pepper to taste
Extra virgin olive oil to taste

Preparation

Clean the quails well, gut them, rinse them in running water, season with salt, pepper, and a drizzle of oil.

Wash and peel the carrots and zucchini, then cut them into sticks.

Divide the vegetables into 4 equal parts for each person and add one quail per serving.

Place the ingredients inside the paper cooking film, add a drizzle of oil and the herbs. Form a bag and close it, tying it well with the string and place it on a oven container.

Preheat the oven to a temperature of 170° C (338° F), put in the oven and cook for 20'. The wrapper will swell, creating steam inside, which will cook the contents evenly while preserving all the aromas.

Serve hot on a plate by opening the bag directly on the table.

Serves
4

Difficulty
Low

Time
10'

Game
Deer

Calories
600 Kcal

Chef
Wade Truong

Wine
Biferno DOC Rosso

COUNTRY FRIED VENISON

Ingredients

G 900 venison loin
G 230 extra fine rice flour
2 eggs
mL 235 milk
mL 150 extra virgin olive oil
G 50 butter
G 50 flour
Salt and pepper to taste

Preparation

Clean the loin, taking care to remove all connective tissue and cut it into medallions about 1 cm thick. Beat the medallions with a meat tenderizer to make them thin, being careful not to tear the meat. You can put the meat between two sheets of plastic wrap to avoid splattering and work from the center of the medallion outwards.

Put the rice flour in a bowl, in another container beat the eggs and milk.

Preheat oil in a frying pan. Season the meat with salt and pepper, dip in the rice flour and shake to remove the excess. Dip the meat in the egg-milk mixture and then dip it again in the rice flour.

Fry one cutlet at a time until the edges are golden brown, about 30-45'', then flip it over to cook the other side for about 30-45''. Remove the meat from the oil and let it drain on a plate with paper towels, and avoid stacking them to keep them crispy. Repeat with the remaining meat.

When it's done, drain the oil from the pan, add equal parts butter and flour to the drippings and make a white gravy, heavy on the black pepper.

Serve with your favorite Southern fixins.

Serves
4

Difficulty
Low

Time
45'

Game
Moose

Calories
383 Kcal

Chef
Gabriel Jonsson

Wine
Salice Salentino DOC Rosato

MOOSE WRAP
WITH YOGURT SAUCE AND PARSLEY OIL

Ingredients

G 400 thin slices of moose
G 15 paprika spice
G 15 Cayenne pepper
G 15 dried thyme
G 15 cumin
G 300 Turkish yogurt
G 10 honey
G 40 grated red cabbage
G 40 finely chopped black cabbage
G 30 arugula
G 10 roasted onion
G 20 pickled red onion
10 cherry tomatoes
1 fist of sunflower sprouts
4-8 tortilla breads
1 lime
1 carrot
1 silver onion
L 1.5 water
mL 800 extra virgin olive oil
1 clove of garlic
Parsley to taste
Thyme, salt and pepper to taste

Preparation

Mix the yogurt, the honey, the thyme, the juice of half lime in a pot; taste with salt and pepper and, if you like, add more lime juice.

For the moose, put oil to a hot frying pan, add the meat and fry until colored. Add the spices – paprika spice, Cayenne pepper, thyme, cumin, salt and pepper – and water. Let simmer a little.

Make a parsley oil by putting the parsley and garlic in a blender, then add 300 mL of oil. Blend until all ingredients are combined, then salt.

Cut the vegetables to the desired size.

Serve everything in a tortilla bread and do not skimp on the sauces or the pickled red onion.

Serves
4

Difficulty
Low

Time
40'

Game
Elk

Calories
300 Kcal

Chef
Michael Hunter

Wine
Primitivo di Manduria DOC

ELK CHILLI

Ingredients

G 500 ground elk meat
mL 750 tomato sauce
1 diced small onion
4 minced cloves of garlic
2 diced stalks of celery
G 180 canned kidney beans white or red
mL 250 stock, game or beef
G 5 ground cumin
G 30 chilli powder
G 5 chilli flakes
G 5 Cayenne pepper
Salt and pepper to taste
Extra virgin olive oil to taste

Optional garnish

Sliced green onion to taste
Sliced jalapeño peppers to taste
Chopped cilantro to taste
Sour cream to taste
Grated cheddar cheese to taste

Preparation

Preheat a medium-size heavy bottom pan on high heat for 3-4'. Add a little oil and add the elk meat. Add a pinch of salt and pepper. Let sauté for 3-4' before stirring to let the meat caramelize and brown.

Stir and let cooking completely. Add the celery, onion and garlic. Stir and cook for 2-3'.

Add the spices, stir and add the tomato, beans and stock.

Cook and simmer for 25-30' on medium in a pot semi-covered with a lid.

Serve hot. You can add the optional garnish, if you like.

CRESCIA FLAKY FLATBREAD
WILD BOAR, CHARD AND CACIOTTA CHEESE

Serves
4

Difficulty
Medium

Time
60'

Game
Wild boar

Calories
920 Kcal

Chef
Iris Rossi

Wine
Rosso Conero DOC

Ingredients

G 200 chopped wild boar
G 200 cooked chard
G 100 finely cut caciotta cheese
2 garlic cloves
1 sprig of rosemary
Salt, coarse salt and pepper to taste
Extra virgin olive oil to taste

For the crescia sfogliata (flatbread)

G 400 '00' flour
2 eggs
G 50 baker's yeast
L 1 milk
G 100 lard
Salt and pepper to taste

Preparation

Crumble the brewer's yeast and dissolve it in the milk. Add salt and pepper to the flour, mix and add the whole eggs, then the yeast dissolved in milk and a small knob of lard. Knead the dough until it becomes smooth and homogeneous.

Form a regular ball, which you will let leaven for a couple of hours. Flour the pastry board, using a rolling pin roll out the dough into a very thin and wide sheet.

Take the rest of the lard, which you have left out of the refrigerator, put a tip on your fingers, and start massaging the dough, leaving an even layer. Roll up the dough, so as to get a long rope of dough (approx. 6 cm large). Take the rope and roll it in the shape of a snail tightly, creating more than one. Let them rest in a cool place for 20'.

Roll out the crescia and cook it, like a flaky flatbread, on a very hot pan, a few minutes each side. Heat the oil, rosemary, and coarse salt in a pan over high heat, pour the chopped wild boar and cook.

Sauté the chard in a pan with oil and a clove of garlic, seasoning with salt. Fill the crescia flatbread with sautéed chard, chopped wild boar and slices of caciotta cheese. Serve hot.

PHEASANT SKEWERS WITH LIME AND MINT

Serves
4

Difficulty
Low

Time
60'

Game
Pheasant

Calories
508 Kcal

Chef
Iris Rossi

Wine
Alta Langa Spumante DOCG

Ingredients

G 400 pheasant breast
G 200 breadcrumbs
2 limes
12 bamboo skewers (15 cm)
12 mint leaves
mL 100 fresh cream
1 lemon
Salt and pepper to taste
Extra virgin olive oil to taste

Preparation

Clean the pheasant breasts thoroughly and cut into strips approx. 2 cm wide along the length of the breast.

Season the breadcrumbs with plenty of oil, salt, freshly ground pepper, grated lime zest and chopped mint.

Bread the pheasant breast strips by pressing the meat in firmly, so that the bread sticks.

Slide strips onto the skewer, threading them over and then under, to create a wave pattern.

Cook on the grill, adding plenty of oil before placing them on the fire.

Season the sour cream with a few drops of lemon and a pinch of salt, taking care that it does not thicken too much.

Serve the skewers hot, alongside a spoonful of sour cream.

Serves
4

Difficulty
Low

Time
30'

Game
Fallow deer

Calories
270 Kcal

Chef
Gabriel Jonsson

Wine
Alto Adige Lagrein DOC

STEWED CHANTERELLE AND VENISON

Ingredients

G 240 thin slices of venison
G 150 chanterelle mushroom
1 chopped shallot
G 150 cranberry
mL 400 cream
mL 15 concentrated chanterelle stock
1 pot of parsley
4 slices of levain bread
G 20 butter
Horseradish to taste
Salt and pepper to taste
Extra virgin olive oil to taste

Preparation

Fry the mushrooms in a pan with a little oil, after cleaning them thoroughly. Add the shallot, a knob of butter and finish cooking.

Put the mushrooms in a bowl.

Heat the meat in a pan with a little oil and pour in the mushrooms. Add the cream and the stock, then simmer. Add salt and pepper to taste.

Add the cranberries almost at the end of the cooking time of the meat, about 2' from the end.

Toast the bread and serve alongside the meat, after covering it with grated horseradish and parsley.

ACKNOWLEDGEMENTS

At the end of this spectacular culinary journey, here we are with the ritual thanks.

Whether directly or otherwise, we want to thank everyone who made the creation of this second volume of recipes possible, and who promoted and supported the project of Franchi Food Academy.

The beauty of traveling is that the end of each journey is just the beginning of the next one... and the next could be just to become a Franchi Food Academy Chef. How?

Passion, creativity and the willingness to get involved, sending of your own recipe to **foodacademy@franchi.com** and who knows... your name might be in the next volume.

#TASTERIGHT

FRANCHI
FEELS RIGHT